customer care

FRANCES AND
ROLAND BEE

INSTITUTE OF PERSONNEL AND DEVELOPMENT

First published in the *Training Extras* series in 1995
Reprinted 1997
First published in the *Management Shapers* series in 1999

Design by Curve
Typesetting by Paperweight
Printed in Great Britain by
The Guernsey Press, Channel Islands

British Library Cataloguing in Publication Data
A catalogue record for this book is available from the
British Library

ISBN
0-85292-776-2

**INSTITUTE OF PERSONNEL
AND DEVELOPMENT**

IPD House, Camp Road, London SW19 4UX
Tel.: 0181 971 9000   Fax: 0181 263 3333
Registered office as above. Registered Charity No. 1038333.
A company limited by guarantee. Registered in England No. 2931892.

customer care

FRANCES AND
ROLAND BEE

Frances and Roland Bee are directors of Time *for* People Ltd, a personnel and training consultancy specialising in customer care, time/self-management, and training needs analysis and evaluation. Together they combine a wide range of professional and management experience in retail, financial services and local authorities. They have worked with a broad range of clients in both the public and private sectors – particularly in retail, transportation, electronics and the universities. Frances and Roland are co-authors of *Management Information Systems and Statistics* (1990), *Training Needs Analysis and Evaluation* (1994), *Project Management* (1997), *Constructive Feedback* (1996), and *Facilitation Skills* (1998), all published by the Institute of Personnel and Development.

Management Shapers is a comprehensive series covering all the crucial management skill areas. Each book includes the key issues, helpful starting points and practical advice in a concise and lively style. Together, they form an accessible library reflecting current best practice – ideal for study or quick reference.

Other titles in the series:

The Institute of Personnel and Development is the leading publisher of books and reports for personnel and training professionals, students, and all those concerned with the effective management and development of people at work. For full details of all our titles please contact the Publishing Department:
tel. 0181-263 3387
fax 0181-263 3850
e-mail publish@ipd.co.uk
The catalogue of all IPD titles can be viewed on the IPD website:
http://www.ipd.co.uk

contents

introduction

This book will be useful to any reader concerned with delivering high-quality customer care, particularly if he or she is:

● intending to design and run a customer care training programme

■ about to attend or has recently attended a customer care programme

▲ studying for a customer care NVQ.

Customer Care provides an *introduction* to the main issues in customer care as well as the opportunity to review the quality of customer care you, your team and organisation currently deliver. It sets out some simple steps you can take and tools you can use to develop and continuously improve the customer care you and your organisation offer. It is based on the philosophy that excellent customer care depends on four fundamental principles, that:

1 the organisation is fully committed to providing excellent customer care and the customer is the key focus throughout the organisation

2   all staff are aware of, and committed to, the vision of excellent customer care

3   all staff are trained to provide the highest-quality customer care

4   systems and procedures are designed to enhance customer care.

The definition of a customer used in this book ranges from the ultimate consumer of the products and services of an organisation, often called the 'external customer', through to everyone in the organisation who is in effect an 'internal customer' for the services and products of other parts of the organisation. *We will show that the quality of customer care offered to internal customers is just as vital as that offered to external customers, and that in successful organisations everyone operates as though all their colleagues are cherished and important customers.*

Chapter 1 looks at why customer care is important to you and your organisation. Chapter 2 examines what is meant by excellent customer care. It looks at the organisation's vision of customer care and then at what customer care means to you. It will help you focus on who your customers are and what products and services you are offering. It will suggest how to set about assessing the quality of customer care you provide. Chapter 3 moves on to the skills of communicating with your customers and how to set about developing positive working relationships – how well you listen to your customers and whether you are asking the right questions. It looks at the issues and skills in communicating face-to-face, by telephone and in writing.

Chapter 4 explores how you find out what your customer needs – what the key aspects of the service are that really matter to the customer. It looks in detail at the vital area of how you deal with complaints and problems. Chapter 5 examines what sort of systems and procedures help you to provide quality customer care, and how well they work. Finally, Chapter 6 focuses on the concept of continuously improving customer care. What can you, your team and organisation do to improve your customer care, and how can you evaluate your progress?

The book provides a structured way of exploring and reviewing the quality of your customer care and how to set about developing and improving it. A number of self-assessments are included – it is important to be honest in order to highlight your strengths and weaknesses. There are a number of exercises – most will take only 15 minutes or so to complete, so try to find the time to do them, because they are important building blocks in the process of understanding and analysing your customer care. The structure provided by the book and the exercises can also be readily adapted to form a training programme. Above all, we hope you will find the book stimulating, and that it will help you reach your goal of delivering excellent customer care.

1 why is customer care important?

Why is customer care important to your organisation?

The answer to this is perhaps obvious, given the number of publications by famous gurus across the world on the subject. One of the earliest disciples of customer care was John Spedan Lewis, founder of the department store and supermarket chain, the John Lewis Partnership, who wrote in 1917:

If we rely upon our value alone we shall obtain considerable success. If to our value we add a constant and careful cultivation of all the other arts of building up and maintaining good will, we shall be vastly more formidable to our Competitors, and do a very great deal better.[1]

In *A Passion for Excellence*, Peters and Austin quote Edson P. Williams, vice-president of the Ford Motor Company:

I'd have to say that (before the events of the last four tough years) our culture in the Ford Motor Company said that there's one central objective in our business, and that's to earn a return on our investment. I think we've now learned there's something else that's central – and that profits will fall to you if you view this as central: Serve the customer. You have to have your costs right, quality right, all those things have to be done. But we must always think the customer is the middle of the thrust of what we're trying to do.[2]

Both these managers have a common focus – that of doing better or achieving higher profits – but they raise two important, if different, issues concerning customer care. Spedan Lewis highlighted the need to differentiate from your competitors and Edson Williams the importance of putting customers at the centre of everything you do. Many would argue that good customer care is essential just to survive and it is exceptional customer care that will set you apart from your competitors. Some organisations talk about customer care as being like the centre of a stick of rock, permeating every part and activity of the organisation. Customer care is not just a set of tasks, a list of dos and don'ts: it is a way of life.

What about some hard evidence? The quality revolution started in manufacturing, where the concept of 'zero defects' was born – the aim of achieving perfect products all of the time. The idea has been extended to customers – with 'zero defections' ie not losing any customers. Research has shown the heavy costs of losing a customer, or rather the future flow of profits lost when a customer 'defects'.[3] The evidence suggests that the profits gained from an individual customer increase significantly over time. These gains come from:

● increased purchasing by the customer over time

- ■ savings from operating costs (as many costs relate to the customer rather than the level of sales)

- ▲ gains from additional customers referred on from a satisfied customer

- ◉ gains from the price premium that people will pay for a service or product that they trust.

The powerful point is made that if you lose a customer it is generally not just that one sale that is lost but potentially a lifetime of sales. Given that it can be very costly to gain a customer, through advertising and other marketing costs, it is perhaps surprising that some organisations are so cavalier in their treatment of customers!

Given the volume of rhetoric and the hard evidence on the importance of retaining and gaining new customers, it would be surprising if most organisations did not subscribe to the belief that customer care was important. However, what distinguishes successful companies is how they turn that belief into a reality. This is what we shall explore with you. We use the word 'explore' deliberately, because we see this book as a journey of discovery about how you and your organisation deliver customer care. We hope that the word also conveys the excitement that comes from a move into unknown territory. Some of you will say: 'This is not unknown territory – we know all about our organisations.' We would say: perhaps for the purposes of reading this book, see the area of customer care as a new world, suspend all your previous assumptions and take an objective look at the quality of customer care that you, your team and your organisation provide.

Why is customer care important to you?

We are making the assumption that if customer care were not important to you, you would not be reading this book. The concept may be important because you are charged with achieving sales or service targets in your job, or because you are responsible for a team and their targets. Maybe it is important because you are trying to gain a qualification, or just because your manager has told you it is important and therefore it *is* important! Perhaps it is important because your job depends on the survival of the organisation and you believe that customer care is a vital element of that survival. However, we would suggest that in addition to these valid reasons for believing customer care is important, there are some other, rather personal (even selfish) reasons:

- Satisfied customers cause less stress. There are few of us who, having had to deal with a dissatisfied customer, do not know the pressures that such situations can bring.

- Satisfied customers take up less time. Dealing with complaints and problems can be very time-consuming, and they always occur when you are at your busiest!

- Satisfied customers tell other people, which enhances your reputation.

- Satisfying customers brings job satisfaction, and can help motivate you and your team.

- Customers are human beings – it's natural to want to provide a service that is courteous, helpful and efficient.

Finally there is the old, but still very relevant, maxim: *your customers are your business*. There is no choice: they are important.

References

1   LEWIS J. S. *Retail Trading: The philosophy and practice of John Spedan Lewis*. London, John Lewis & Co. Ltd, 1979.

2   PETERS T. J. *and* AUSTIN N. *A Passion for Excellence: The leadership difference*. Glasgow, Fontana, 1986.

3   REICHHELD F. F. *and* SASSER W. E. JNR. 'Zero defections: quality comes to services'. *Harvard Business Review*, Sept–Oct 1990.

2 what is excellent customer care?

What is the organisation's vision of customer care?

In the Introduction we said that two of the four fundamental principles of excellent customer care are that:

- the organisation is fully committed to providing excellent customer care and the customer is the key focus throughout the organisation

- all staff are aware of, and committed to, the vision of excellent customer care.

Many organisations set out their vision of the future in the form of vision or mission statements backed up by what are often called 'core values'. These are intended to set out for customers, staff, suppliers etc what the organisation wants to achieve and how it wants to achieve it. For example, Eastern Electricity sets out its vision in this way:

The Eastern Group will provide a quality of service in the energy and network management sectors which will make it the customers' choice.[1]

This is backed up by four main core values, of which the first is:

BELIEF IN SERVING OUR CUSTOMERS

As part of our quality process we will:

- *continue to develop a partnership with our customers*
- *anticipate and meet the changing needs of our customers so that we are their supplier of choice.*[1]

Another example, from the financial services sector, is a vision statement:

To be the most successful information service company world-wide by enabling our customers to harness the power of information.

This is backed up by a values statement on customer care:

Our aim is always to exceed the expectations of our customers. In doing so we treat every customer as if they were the largest and manage every aspect of our service as if it were the most important.

These are the mechanisms by which organisations make public commitments to the quality of service they want to provide. It is the vital first step on the path towards excellent customer care. For the vision and value statements to provide the driving force there are three further important steps:

1   Everyone in the organisation needs to be aware of, and be committed to, that vision and those values.

2 The vision and values must be translated into action.

3 The vision and values must be translated into measurable targets for customer care performance so that organisations can monitor and review their achievements.

Examples of the ways organisations approach Step 1 are by:

● providing half-day road shows for staff, targeted at large groups of staff and involving senior management, aimed at getting a consistent message across quickly

■ cascading the information down through team briefings

▲ using videos, newsletters etc.

Examples of the ways organisations approach Step 2 are by:

● carrying out research to find out what customers need and what they think of the service they receive

■ running training programmes for staff in customer care

▲ running training programmes to ensure staff are competent to do their jobs

● reviewing processes and procedures to ensure they are customer-focused.

Examples of the ways organisations approach Step 3 are by:

- setting clear performance targets for teams and individuals so that everyone is clear exactly what service standard they are aiming for

- monitoring and acting on the results.

Take a sheet of paper and try Exercise 1.

Exercise 1

1 Does your organisation have a vision or mission statement and a supporting set of values?
   – *Yes/No/Don't Know*

   If 'Yes', what are they? What are the parts that relate to customer care?

   If 'Don't Know', find out!

2 How did you find out about the mission/value statements?

3 Do you feel that the organisation is committed to customer care?
   – *Yes/No*

   Explain the reasons for your answer.

What does customer care mean to you?

Probably the best way of understanding what customer care means to you is to think of your experiences as a customer. We are all customers for some service or product almost all of the time. It is often easier at this stage to think of examples outside work – travelling on the local transport system, shopping at a supermarket, as a parent of a child receiving an education, eating in a local Indian restaurant, having your refrigerator repaired or boiler serviced. The list is endless. Exercise 2 asks you to think of two examples of good and bad customer care, and to recall what factors contributed to these experiences. In this way you can begin to identify the sort of things that make a customer interaction an example of excellent or poor customer care. The exercise also asks you to remember the experience as fully as possible in terms of your feelings at the time and, finally, how you feel now about the experience.

Try Exercise 2 overleaf. Take your time: being able to put yourself in the customer's shoes, see things from their perspective, hear through their ears and experience their feelings are all part of a vital step towards your delivering excellent customer care. This is a very useful exercise for anyone involved in customer care – therefore, given our definition of a customer, this means that everyone in the organisation should do it! Encourage other team members to have a go. The exercise is also a very good starting-point for customer care training. It usually runs best if delegates work in small groups first, then report back to the full group.

Exercise 2

During the past year there will have been many occasions when you will have been a customer for either products or services. Think of:

○ two examples of what you regard as **excellent** customer care

▢ two examples of what you regard as **poor** customer care.

For each example:

○ identify the key factors that contributed to the experiences
▢ describe your feelings and reactions at the time
△ describe your feelings and reactions now.

Example 1 Excellent Customer Care	*Example 2* Excellent Customer Care
Describe briefly the circumstances:	Describe briefly the circumstances:
List the factors that contributed to this being an excellent customer care experience:	List the factors that contributed to this being an excellent customer care experience:
My feelings and reactions at the time:	My feelings and reactions at the time:
My feelings and reactions now:	My feelings and reactions now:

Example 1 Poor Customer Care	Example 2 Poor Customer Care
Describe briefly the circumstances:	Describe briefly the circumstances:
List the factors that contributed to this being a poor customer care experience:	List the factors that contributed to this being a poor customer care experience:
My feelings and reactions at the time:	My feelings and reactions at the time:
My feelings and reactions now:	My feelings and reactions now:

Typically, the sort of *factors* that tend to emerge with surprising consistency are those described in the table on page 18.

Factors contributing to excellent customer care	Factors contributing to poor customer care
⊙ Knowledgeable and professional staff.	⊙ Nobody had a clue about anything.
▣ Friendly and courteous staff, even when under pressure.	▣ Nobody seemed interested or bothered.
△ Staff were helpful, but not pushy.	△ They fobbed me off – it was always somebody else's job or fault.
⊙ They listened to me.	⊙ They treated me as though I was a fool/liar.
⊙ They took responsibility.	
⊙ They did what they said they would.	⊙ They behaved as if it was *my* fault.
▣ They kept me informed – I didn't have to chase.	⊙ They were always late/never turned up when they said they would.
△ They seemed to care.	
⊙ They responded promptly to my enquiry/problem.	▣ I had to chase all the time.
⊙ They seemed to be proud of their product/service/ organisation.	△ They were always complaining about their colleagues/the management/ organisation.

Typically, people's *reactions* towards these experiences are very similar, as the table opposite outlines.

Reactions to excellent customer care	Reactions to poor customer care
○ I felt really pleased and happy.	○ I felt upset.
▣ I felt cared about.	▣ I felt very angry.
△ I trusted them.	△ I felt humiliated.
○ I looked forward to using their services again.	○ I felt powerless.
○ I wanted to tell everyone how good they were.	○ I vowed never to use them again.
	○ I wanted to let the whole world know how awful they were.

What is often surprising is how long these reactions last. The message that comes across is that good/bad customer care can arouse powerful emotions and result in some remarkable benefits or disastrous consequences. Not only is there the opportunity to retain or lose the customer concerned, there is also the opportunity to gain or lose several more. Research shows that someone who has had a bad customer experience will tell at least 10 other people!

It is useful to repeat the exercise, this time taking examples from within the workplace – where you have been an internal customer for colleagues' services or products. The results usually turn out to be much the same. However, the strategies people adopt in response to *poor* service are a little different. You might argue that, as an internal customer, you are a captive customer: you cannot take your custom elsewhere. However, people will often try to do the equivalent – ie they find ways around the difficult or unhelpful colleague by perhaps going to someone else in the team; doing without that service by, for example, taking care of their own photocopying; or going without a certain piece of information. The net effect is detrimental to the efficient and effective working of the organisation. Ultimately the end customer suffers. The response to telling everyone what has happened is exactly the same – it is very easy to get a reputation for being unhelpful, never delivering the goods on time, not knowing what you are doing. Equally, but perhaps not so easily, achievable is the goal of being regarded as a valued and competent member of the team, someone it is a pleasure to deal with. How would *you* like to be regarded?

Who are your customers?

As you start off on what you might now be regarding as the perilous path of delivering excellent customer care, with the green fields and sunshine of success on the one side and the wasteland and rain of failure on the other, the obvious first question to address is: who are your customers? It is pretty hard to deliver good customer care unless you know exactly who they are. In some cases the answer may appear fairly simple. If you are a waiter, your main customers are clearly the people that present themselves at your tables. However, what about customers on other tables, on their way in and out, or those ringing to book a table, or to complain? What about your internal customers – your colleagues in the

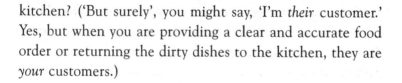

kitchen? ('But surely', you might say, 'I'm *their* customer.' Yes, but when you are providing a clear and accurate food order or returning the dirty dishes to the kitchen, they are *your* customers.)

The key to identifying your customers is to think of a typical day or week, and to jot down whom you have contact with – face-to-face, on the telephone or in writing. Then think about the purpose of that interaction – are they a customer for your services or products? You are now ready to fill in Part 1 of Exercise 3 (see page 24). If you are a team leader, you might decide to answer on behalf of yourself or the team as a whole. You might also consider making copies of Exercise 3 and getting all your team members to fill one in. It is a good exercise to use on a training programme. When you design your own version of the exercise, remember to allow adequate space for the comments.

What products and services are you providing?

Having identified your customers, the next stage is to think about your products and services. For example, if you are in retail on the shop floor, your main customers are probably members of the public; the services you personally offer include providing information, taking orders, taking payment and wrapping goods. Some of your internal customers could include the cash office, for whom the service you offer is cashing up the till; the clerks, for whom it is completing special order forms; and the store detectives, for whom it is alerting them to suspicious occurrences. Also, what about your colleagues on the shop floor – what is the service you offer them? It may include being alert to help out when they are busy, or ensuring that you are back from your breaks so that the next person can go to their break on time. In an office, you may be supplying information to a wide range of different colleagues inside and outside your own team; or you may be responsible for ensuring the computer equipment is working and, if not, taking the appropriate action. As a trainer, you may be providing a service of training in particular skill and knowledge areas to the trainees, and liaising with clients for the training to ensure that the right sort is delivered.

Are you ready to fill in Part 2 of Exercise 3? Think hard and be as precise as possible about what you are doing for your customers.

What is the quality of the customer care you provide?

You are entering the last stage of your journey exploring the customer care that you currently provide. Having identified your customers and the nature of the service or product you offer, the final crucial question is how well you do it – what is the quality of the customer care you are providing at the moment? There are usually four crucial elements involved in delivering quality customer care:

● *appropriateness*: is your service/product what the

customer actually wants – does it precisely meet their needs?

■ *consistency/reliability*: is your service/product of the required standard all the time?

▲ *timeliness*: do you provide the service when the customer needs it, over a reasonable time period?

● *satisfying*: does the way you provide your service ensure that it is a good experience for the customer, eg are you friendly and helpful, do you show interest and/or concern?

You are now ready to complete Part 3 of Exercise 3. Think about the quality of the services you offer your customers, and give yourself, or your team, a rating. Try to be as honest as possible. You might like to consider asking your customers what *they* think. Here are some suggestions how you might do it:

● Talk to them informally next time you are in contact.

■ Set up a meeting with some or all of your customers specifically to discuss their views on the service you offer.

▲ Design a short questionnaire seeking their views.

Reference

1 EASTERN ELECTRICITY. *Roadshow Reminders*. 1994 (unpublished).

Exercise 3

1 List your customers – it is helpful to try to list them in terms of frequency of contact (ie in order of the number of times you deal with that customer) and indicate whether they are external (E) or internal (I) customers.

2 Describe briefly the nature of the product/service you are providing.

3 Indicate the quality of service you offer at present, using a scale from 1 to 6, where 1 = very poor quality and 6 = excellent quality. You might wish to add some comments explaining the ratings.

1 Who are my customers?	E/I	2 What is the service/product?	3 What is the quality of service?

communicating with your customers

How we communicate

There is one skill that runs through every aspect of working life: the ability to communicate effectively. It is at the heart of excellent customer care and is central to developing positive working relationships with your customers. You communicate with your customers in one of three ways:

● face-to-face – in your shop, office or factory, or when you go out to their homes or offices

■ on the telephone – responding to their calls or initiating calls yourself

▲ in writing – by letter, memo, report, circular, etc.

There are some basic rules that apply to all forms of communication, and then there are some specific skills that go with each type of communication. The first basic rule concerns how we communicate. A number of researchers have looked at this. One of the most famous is Albert Mehrabian, who came up with some fascinating results. He concluded that the way a message is conveyed is through:

● *what* we say ie the words we use – 7 per cent

- *how* we say it ie use of the voice in terms of tone, volume, pace – 38 per cent

- our *body language* – 55 per cent.[1]

An interesting exercise in a training programme is to ask people to guess the percentages. Most people assume that the words we use are the most important part of our communication; this is perhaps not surprising, because we spend a lot of time thinking about what we are going to say – 'choosing the right words'. Words in their own right can be very confusing – think about the three different meanings of the word 'coke' (a coal derivative; slang for 'cocaine'; a sugary drink)! There is also the increasing problem of abbreviations eg APL, TQM, KPI. The first two are widely used – Accredited Prior Learning and Total Quality Management; the third is a company abbreviation – Key Performance Indicator. The careless use of abbreviations can seriously hamper effective communication. We remember attending a conference on car crime where the abbreviation IT was constantly used. Our usual understanding of IT, that it stands for Information Technology, did not seem to make much sense. It turned out to stand for Intermediate Treatment. Any the wiser? This is a good example of another problem area for words: that of jargon – Intermediate Treatment is an alternative punishment to 'custodial sentences'. You can imagine how this confusion affected our understanding of the presentation! Customers can often find abbreviations and jargon intimidating as well as baffling, so use both with care and, when in doubt, always explain.

Few would deny that most of us underestimate the potential of our voice for aiding communication. The phrase 'I am sorry, we are out of stock' can convey at least three different messages, depending on how it is said. It can convey that you really are very sorry you do not have what the customer wants; it can convey that you could not care less what the customer wants; and, worst of all, it can convey irritation – 'Surely it's obvious why there are no items on display!' The message is conveyed through the emphasis you put on different words, the volume of the voice, the pace of speech and the general tone. Unless we concentrate hard, our voice will accurately reflect how we are truly feeling. If we are sorry, generally we shall sound sorry; if we are irritated, then we shall sound irritated. What Mehrabian proved, and what we all know from experience, is that the message which gets across is the underlying one carried by our voice, and it does not matter too much what words are used. Voice becomes even more important on the telephone, when the third medium of communication, body language, is of course not available.

Body language is the most important medium of communication. A simple and powerful example is the expression on your face: do you look happy and cheerful, or miserable, or angry? Smiling is an amazingly effective way of initiating and maintaining effective communication. (Although obviously only when it is appropriate: it may not be too helpful if a customer is telling you that the computer you sold them has just crashed, destroying all their files!)

Eye contact also plays a very large part. Get someone to try an experiment with you: ask them whether they had a nice weekend or holiday. First do it looking over their shoulder or out of the window and then do it looking fully at them. Ask them how they felt. Universally, people will say that whereas in the first case they felt you were not interested in what they were saying, in the second case they felt you were. Generally, eye contact is very helpful – but do not overdo it. If you stare fixedly at someone it can make them feel very uncomfortable!

The whole stance of your body can convey powerful messages. Contrast how you stand or sit when you are feeling very confident with how you do so when you are feeling nervous or unhappy. You hear the phrase that someone looks 'dejected' or 'down'. Generally, when you are feeling confident you sit or stand upright, with your shoulders back, but when you are feeling low your shoulders will be hunched and you will tend to look down rather than up. These are instinctive reactions of your body to how you feel. Interestingly, and helpfully, it can work the other way: when you are feeling nervous try sitting more upright and looking ahead. This has two advantages: your posture may suggest to others that you feel confident even if you do not, but more usefully it may actually make you feel more confident.

Body language is a very complex subject and many people now argue that you cannot make generalised interpretations, because everyone has their own body language. What is important, however, is to observe very carefully other people's body language and learn to interpret it. In the same way that you are conveying powerful messages through your body language, so you can also pick up valuable information about how your customer is feeling, and react accordingly. Later we shall discuss strategies for dealing with difficult customer situations – where the customer is perhaps angry, nervous or upset.

Whenever we communicate we must always be prepared to cater for people with special needs eg impaired sight or hearing, people for whom English is not their first language, or perhaps people with dyslexia. These customers represent a special challenge and opportunity to demonstrate your high levels of customer care.

We are going to concentrate now on three key communication skills:

● building and maintaining rapport

■ active listening

▲ effective questioning.

Building and maintaining rapport

This is the vital skill that sets the foundation for all effective communication. Unless you achieve and maintain rapport, effective communication is unlikely to take place. So what do we mean by this curious term 'rapport'? The dictionary definition is 'achieving a harmonious and understanding relationship'. However, try asking people what it means to them – colleagues, members of your team or delegates on a customer care training programme. The sorts of answer you are likely to get are:

- feeling at ease or comfortable with someone
- getting alongside people
- getting on the same wavelength
- feeling empathy with people
- seeing eye-to-eye with people.

We talked in Chapter 2 about the ability to put yourself in the customers' shoes – to see events and circumstances from their perspective, hear it through their ears and experience their feelings. When you have achieved rapport then this will happen almost automatically. The advantages are two-fold: it is much easier to provide the quality of customer care that customers want if you know exactly how they perceive and feel about a situation; also, by taking the trouble to enter and understand the customers' world, you are demonstrating that you have time for them and see them as important.

Some find it quite easy to get into rapport with people, whereas others find that it does not come naturally. Also, even those that are skilled in achieving rapport will occasionally meet people with whom it is more difficult. The skill has a lot to do with observing and listening to people very closely. For example, if you are dealing with a customer who is very softly spoken, it is helpful if you also speak softly. If the customer speaks quite loudly and directly, a similar response will suggest to the customer that you communicate in a similar way. It is like tuning into the same frequency on a radio.

The way you feel influences your body language, so matching someone else's body language can give a very useful insight into how that person is feeling. You are also joining them in their world. However, this must be done with care (a little goes a long way!) because there would be nothing worse than for someone to feel they were being mimicked. First, try observing people in social situations – you will often see that close friends engaged in conversation have very similar body language – in terms of the tilt of the head, body posture, use of arms and hands etc. Then try to match other people's voice and body language in social situations – see whether you feel it improves the quality of the relationship and of communication.

Active listening

We are taught how to talk and how to write, but nobody teaches us to listen. You may say it is something we do naturally. However, our ability to listen effectively is often very limited. Try listening to a tape of someone talking for 2 or 3 minutes without making any notes. Then jot down how

Exercise 4

WHERE DOES PAUL LIVE?*

Instructions

1 Work in pairs role-playing a telephone conversation by sitting back-to-back.
2 The *speaker* reads the passage below, aloud and once only.
3 The *speaker* cannot be interrupted or asked to repeat points.
4 The *listener* listens to the main points and puts these in logical order.
5 The *listener* cannot take notes.

'Turn left at the roundabout, where the pub is – you know, the one that has the bouncers at the door. What's it called now? Oh, that's right, the Cock and Bull. Right miserable landlord. There was a big punch-up there last week and one of the bouncers got pushed through a window. But not many people rushed to help him.

'So, go along the road and up the hill. If you go left there, that's where the old pop star lives. You know, the one that used to wear all those glittering suits. What was his name? Oh, never mind.

'Carry straight on then, and at the top take the right fork, by the big tree – I think it's an oak. Or is it an acorn tree? I don't know – I hated nature walks at school. Stay on that road till you pass the big white house with the swimming pool. My aunt lives next door to that, in the little cottage. She works at the cinema now, you know, and she reckons she might be able to get some free tickets...

'Anyway, past the house. Acacia Avenue is first on the right and Paul lives at number eight – or is it ten? No, it is ten, same as the Prime Minister's.'

Feedback

1 The *listener* repeats to the *speaker* what he or she has understood to be the main points, in logical order.
2 The *speaker* checks the *listener's* accuracy.
3 The *listener* lists all the difficulties he or she experienced in this activity.

*Based on Activity 8 in *Communications Workshop: A manual*[2]

much you can remember: you may be surprised at how much you have missed. Try Exercise 4 with friends or colleagues, or use it on a training programme.

What we refer to as *active* listening is very hard. It involves:

● being attentive and showing it eg by maintaining eye contact well, nodding your head

■ listening not just to what is said but how it is said

▲ absorbing and interpreting the non-verbal messages

● making the effort not just to hear but to *understand*

● reflecting back and summarising – using your own words to repeat back what you have heard so you can check you have got the correct message.

It is very obvious when someone is not listening. If you recall when this has happened to you, you will probably remember feeling a sense of rejection: the person was not interested in what you had to say. Often in these circumstances you stop trying to communicate, and the relationship can be adversely affected. Active listening is an essential component of maintaining rapport. The difference between hearing and listening has been described in these terms: hearing is a physical activity whereas listening is a cognitive/thinking ability. In other words, to listen you have to use your thought processes in order to translate the message and understand it.

There can be many barriers to active listening. The obvious ones are being distracted by other noises or events around you. However, there are a great number of more subtle barriers that interfere with listening, for example when:

● you think that you know what the other person is going to say – the risk is that it is very easy either to stop listening altogether or hear only what you want, or expect, to hear. If a customer has a regular order of 100 black boxfiles you may not pick up the fact that the order is for *red* boxfiles this month. The golden rule is not to make assumptions.

■ you are waiting to have your say – how many times in meetings, when you are very anxious to make your point, do you suddenly realise you have missed whole chunks of what has been said by other people?

▲ you are bored – your mind will wander on to more interesting things!

- you are thinking about something else – your mind is on an imminent, possibly unpleasant, meeting with a dissatisfied customer.

- you are in a hurry – your thoughts will focus on trying to finish the conversation, not on what is being communicated.

- you are angry – you will probably stop listening carefully to what other people are saying.

- you are tired, thirsty or hungry, or you are feeling hot or cold – physical discomfort can be a powerful barrier to listening, because the feelings of thirst or heat etc, and ways of relieving them, will dominate your thoughts.

Sometimes it is difficult to overcome these barriers. However, there are some simple principles that may help. If you are discussing an issue with a customer, try to ensure that:

- you can talk somewhere quiet without being disturbed

- the situation is comfortable but not as relaxing as in a sauna!

- you clear your mind of other issues and concentrate solely on the customer and the matter in hand

- you allow enough time

- you keep an open mind and do not make assumptions

- you stay calm.

A guide to effective questioning

Type of information required	Useful questions
Full information on a customer's needs, or a problem that has arisen.	Ask *open* questions: these encourage the customer to provide a lot of information. They usually begin with 'how', 'what', 'why', 'where', 'who' and 'when', or 'tell me about…' Use pauses – they allow the customer time to think, and prevent the discussion becoming an interrogation.
Detailed information on a particular aspect of a customer's needs or problems.	Ask *probing* questions: 'What *specifically* did the engineer say to you when…?'; 'Tell me in *detail* about the fault on the knob…'; '*Exactly* what happened after you returned to the department on the second occasion?'
Confirmation or denial of a point, or a specific piece of information.	Ask *closed* questions: these result in a yes/no or one-word answer – 'Did you tell customers at the point of sale that they must retain the bill as proof of purchase?'; 'What time did you receive the order details?'

Effective questioning

The third key skill is the ability to ask effective questions. Delivering excellent customer care depends on having the right information. Getting at the right information quickly is a skill that can be developed. It depends on what sort of information you are trying to obtain. The table opposite provides some guidance on useful questions to ask – open, probing, and closed questions – and on using pauses.

There are also two types of question to avoid:

- *leading questions*. As the name suggests, these lead the respondent into specific answers. For example: 'You did tell the customer that their order would not be in until after Christmas, didn't you?'

- *multiple questions*. For example: 'What happened when you turned the oven on and set the timer?' Multiple questions can be confusing: are you looking for two separate pieces of information, or do you want to know what happened after the customer had both turned the oven on and set the timer?

Whereas open questions are sometimes surprisingly difficult to formulate, it is all too easy to slip into closed questions at inappropriate times and to ask leading questions etc. Try Exercise 5 (overleaf), working with two colleagues. It is a fun exercise to use in a training programme.

Exercise 5

QUESTIONING SKILLS

Choose a topic that will interest you and one of your colleagues eg a holiday or a particular aspect of work. Spend five minutes questioning your colleague, but try to use open and probing questions only. Your other colleague will observe and monitor what sorts of question you ask – open, probing, closed, multiple or leading. Change roles, so that each of you has a turn at asking the questions, being questioned, and observing.

Achieving excellent communication skills takes effort and energy. (It is particularly hard to achieve if you are stressed or under pressure.) Individuals who excel at customer care are willing to expend that effort and energy on *every* occasion they deal with a customer.

So far we have looked at communication skills in general and at those which are particularly relevant to face-to-face situations. We now look at other types of communication with customers – on the telephone and in writing.

Dealing with customers on the telephone

The most obvious feature of dealing with customers on the telephone is that you miss out on the very valuable information you otherwise give and receive through body language. Therefore this puts more emphasis not only on the words you use but also, even more importantly, on how you use your voice. Here are some useful tips:

- You may have heard the phrase 'Put a smile in your voice.' This is easy to do: simply smile as you speak on the telephone.

- If you know the person, try visualising them and speak as if they were sitting opposite you.

- If you want to sound authoritative or firm, try standing as you speak on the telephone.

- Listen actively not just to *what* is said but *how* it is said – does the caller sound rushed, irritated or relaxed? – and respond accordingly. For example, if someone is in a hurry, it is not helpful to sound as though you have all the time in the world. Most people who feel rushed will talk quite fast, so try matching their pace of speaking. If, however, you feel it would be helpful to take more time, then gradually slow your pace. It is all about being sensitive to whom you are speaking and being willing to take the time and trouble to get, and stay, alongside them.

There are two telephone situations – receiving a customer's call and initiating a call. In either case, there are some simple techniques you can use. Think first about *receiving* calls:

- Be prepared: have a pen, notepad or message pad ready. *Always* make a note of the call.

- Answer the phone as quickly as possible. Some

organisations set service standards such as 'all calls to be answered within three rings'. This can be particularly important if the call has come through a switchboard.

▲ Give the call your full attention: put other work aside. If you do not, you will stop listening actively and may miss vital information – and the caller will soon notice. This is not likely to make them feel valued!

◉ Smile before you speak, and say 'Good morning/afternoon.'

◉ Introduce yourself – by name and perhaps department and/or organisation. Some organisations have a standard form of introduction. If this is the case, it is important to make your introduction sound personal and sincere on each occasion. We have probably all experienced the sing-song voice saying, 'Good morning, this is Pat speaking, how can I help you?' There are advantages to telling staff what information should be included, but let people decide for themselves exactly how it is said.

◉ Remember the 90:90 rule: you make 90 per cent of your impression in the first 90 seconds of the call, so be ready right from the start to give it your best.

◼ Find out the caller's name and use it. This personalises the communication.

▲ Use your skills to build and maintain rapport, listen actively and question effectively.

● Try to deal with the call yourself: callers find being passed on to someone else frustrating.

● If you have to transfer a call: explain why and what you are doing; to whom the call is being transferred, and the extension number (in case the call gets lost); and ensure you are transferring the call to the *right* place. Many phone systems allow you to speak to the person to whom you are transferring the call: it is useful to check that the person can deal with the call, and to provide brief background information on it.

● If you have to put a call on hold for any reason, explain why, and offer the caller the alternative of being called back; check back regularly, so the caller knows they have not been forgotten.

■ If you need to phone the caller back, agree when you will do it – and make sure you do!

▲ When you end the call, summarise any action that has been agreed and check the caller is happy with the outcome. It is courteous to thank them for calling.

● Afterwards, take any necessary follow-up action. If you have taken a message for someone else, make sure you pass it on quickly.

Many of these techniques are identical for *initiating* a call. However, this time you have more control and can plan, so in addition to the previous points:

● Prepare by thinking about: what the purpose of the call is and what outcome you want to achieve; whom you need to speak to and, if they are not available, whether anyone else can help; which main points you want to cover, and what questions to ask; what questions you might be asked.

■ Think some more about whom you are going to call: have you dealt with them before? Prepare mentally how best to establish rapport.

▲ Remember, again, the 90:90 rule: the initial moments of the call are the most important.

● Always check that it is a convenient time to call: it is often useful to indicate how much time you will need eg say whether it is just a quick call to check some detail, or to discuss a complex situation or to obtain a lot of information.

If you or your team use the telephone often, you might decide to display these tips in a clear and eye-catching form in a prominent position. Even better, try getting your team to come up with their own list: people are usually more committed to ideas or techniques they themselves have helped devise. It gives them a sense of ownership. You can also devise a check-list for people to review their own performance on the telephone.

Writing to customers

If you are writing to a customer, the required ingredients are the same as those for all aspects of customer care:

- The communication must be timely. Indeed, many organisations set performance standards eg all customer letters replied to within three days, all orders confirmed within 24 hours, customers to be updated on their orders weekly.

- The communication must be accurate. Written communication is a very precise and unforgiving method of communication: your mistakes are recorded in black and white for posterity!

These are what we would describe as necessary but not, in themselves, sufficient requirements for excellent customer communication. The 'extra' is the way the letter, memo or report is written. It is useful at this point to consider the differences between written and other forms of communication. (This makes a valuable exercise in a training programme.) The main characteristics about *written communication* are that:

- you have more time to plan what you are going to say

- the communication is one-way: there is no opportunity to check for understanding, to observe how the other person is reacting, and therefore no opportunity to explain or refine the message

▲ you have to rely solely on the power of your words. That meagre 7 per cent of the message accounted for by the medium of words in face-to-face communication must now account for the full 100 per cent.

● it provides a permanent record

● you cannot be sure that the message is received unless you use a system such as recorded delivery or return slips, or check personally

● it is a less immediate form of communication: there is always some time gap.

It is the first three characteristics above that provide the key to the way the letter or memo etc should be written, and of those three the first is the most important. You have the opportunity to *plan* the communication, so use it! Consider:

● *whom* you are writing to. Is it an external customer or someone within the organisation? What is their level of understanding of the issues, jargon etc? What is your relationship with them – how formal or informal should the communication be?

■ *why* you are writing. What is the purpose of the communication?

▲ *when* you should write. How urgent is it? When would be an appropriate time?

● *what* you should write. What does the customer need to

know? What information do *you* need? What points must you cover?

Then remember the 'Five Cs'. Be:

1   *clear* – does the letter etc follow a logical sequence? Will it be understood? You will have no opportunity to check as you go along that your correspondent understands your message, therefore it is important to be clear and unambiguous. Before you send it, ask somebody else to read it and then check what their understanding is.

2   *concise* – people are usually short of time, so make the letter brief and to the point.

3   *courteous* – is it too formal or informal? Have you thanked or apologised as appropriate? Think about the words you use: avoid sounding officious, patronising or uninterested. *Does your letter show you value the customer and care about their needs?*

4   *complete* – have you covered all the necessary points? (Refer back to your plan.)

5   *correct* – is your information accurate and up to date? Are there any mistakes in spelling (use the spell check in your word processor), punctuation or grammar?

Finally, remember that every communication with a customer is a golden opportunity to develop a positive relationship with that person. Jan Carlson of SAS Airlines described these opportunities as 'moments of truth'. Excellent customer care is about ensuring these opportunities are used to the full on every occasion, whatever the circumstances.

References

1   MEHRABIAN A. *and* FERRIS L. 'Inference of attitudes from nonverbal communication in two channels'. *The Journal of Counselling Psychology*. Vol 31, 1967. pp248–52

2   BECKETT C., TIDY D., ROGERS O., *and* WATERMAN M. *Communications Workshop: A manual*. Oxford, Heinemann, 1989.

4 meeting customer needs

It may seem obvious to state that meeting customer needs is at the core of excellent customer care. Surely, that is what the whole business is about: there is no interaction unless you are supplying something the customer needs. The customer goes to the garage because he or she needs petrol, goes to the doctor because he or she needs to be well, goes on the train because he or she needs to get from A to B, gets information on outstanding invoices because he or she needs it to do his or her job. However, is it that simple? What distinguishes customer interactions that the customer would describe as providing excellent customer care from those that are mediocre or even poor? What are the customer's basic or minimum needs and what else might be important to the customer? Let's look at each in turn in the table on page 48.

Customer Interaction	Minimum Need	Additional Needs
Goes to the garage for petrol.	Petrol of the type required available, with an acceptable length of queue.	Forecourt clean and tidy. Paper towels for cleaning hands. Friendly and prompt service. Good lighting at night.
Goes to the doctor because of illness.	To see a competent doctor/nurse and receive appropriate treatment.	Not waiting too long. Comfortable waiting-room. Pleasant, helpful receptionist. Doctor/nurse who establishes a good relationship and makes you feel cared about.
Travels on the train.	To get from A to B at the times set out in the timetable.	Not too long a queue at the ticket office. Pleasant, helpful service at the ticket office. Ticket machines that work. Clean, comfortable train. Seat available and train not too crowded. Good, clear announcements. Kept informed if there are problems.
Receives report on outstanding invoices.	Receives report on time, with accurate/up-to-date information.	Report laid out in a clear and helpful way. Kept informed if there are any problems. Friendly and helpful response to any queries on the report. Quick response to any queries.

The minimum need is the obvious part, or at least it should be. However, there is room for discussion about this: should part of the minimum need at the doctor's be not to wait too long, should part of the minimum service travelling on a train be to have a seat? The answer may vary. For example, on a long-distance journey you may expect a seat, although you may not on a commuter-length journey. What is a 'reasonable' wait at the doctor's surgery?

The additional needs are even less obvious. All the examples in the table are ones you are likely to have experienced in some form recently. What is important to you when you go to a garage, the doctor, travel on the train, receive information from colleagues? Try using these and other examples at team briefing sessions or during customer care training.

In Chapter 2 we asked you to review the services you offer to your customers, both inside and outside the organisation, and how you rated the quality in general terms. Now we are going to look at quality of service in detail. If you have ever worked in retail you will probably have heard the saying 'retail is detail'. The saying is equally relevant to customer care: it is often attention to detail that characterises excellent customer care. However, first you have to find out what matters to your customers. Perhaps the best way is to ask them; putting yourself in their shoes is also useful – try being a customer for your team's or organisation's services.

Organisations use a variety of ways to try to get at this information eg:

- surveys of customer needs – using either self-complete questionnaires or interviews

- customer panels – who are consulted regularly about their needs and satisfaction with the services provided

- customer focus groups – held with eg a major customer, or a group of customers, where there are detailed discussions on the best fit of the services to that customer (these can apply to both external and internal customers)

- customer comment cards – of the type found in hotel bedrooms, which are aimed primarily at information on customer satisfaction with the services received, but can also provide invaluable information on customer needs eg for a quiet room, vegetarian meals etc

- customer hotline – a freephone for customers to ring in with views on the service they need or have received.

Clearly, the information from these sources needs to be captured in a way that allows it to be stored, analysed and retrieved as necessary, so trends can be established and patterns identified for action.

In their best-seller, *In Search of Excellence*, Peters and Waterman listed getting 'close to the customer' as one of the eight key attributes that distinguished 'excellent, innovative companies':

These companies learn from the people they serve. They provide unparalleled quality, service, and reliability… Everybody gets in on the act. Many of the innovative companies got their best product ideas from customers. That comes from listening, intently and regularly.[1]

Often the best information will come from people who are on the front line – those who interact directly with the customer. It is important to:

- encourage people to listen actively to their customers throughout the process of providing the service, to be alert and receptive to comments, proposals and ideas

- encourage staff to seek information from their customers, to ask their views

- provide effective ways of ensuring the information collected in this way is communicated to the appropriate part of the organisation so that it can be acted upon.

Use Exercise 6 (overleaf) to look in detail at two areas of service you or your team offer. This provides a useful exercise in a training programme or may form the basis of a lively team-briefing session.

Exercise 6

Choose two areas of customer service that you or your team
provide:

- ⊙ What is the minimum customer need?
- ▢ What are the additional customer needs?
- △ How well do you meet those needs?

Customer service area	Minimum need	Additional needs	How well you meet those needs

---

It is important regularly to check your perception and
understanding of customer needs – they will change
continuously. There is little doubt that customers'
expectations of the service they receive are increasing all
the time. At a simple level, it may be for facilities like free
car-parking right next to the supermarket. At a more complex
level, expectations in terms of promptness, reliability and
courteous service are rising too. The rule is never to be
complacent. Don't assume you know: check continuously
with the people who do know – your customers.

One of the most fertile areas for learning about and
understanding customers' needs is their complaints.

Handling customer complaints

Customer complaints are a two-edged sword. On the one hand, they are used as a measure of poor customer service, but on the other hand they are a priceless source of information on customers' needs and expectations. Although this may appear strange, increasingly organisations see getting complaints as a good thing. It is often quoted that for every complaint you receive, there are 20 other customers who do not bother to complain – they just remove their custom. Receiving a complaint at least provides the opportunity to do something about it. If you do not receive the complaint there is nothing you can do to put matters right. A customer complaint provides a golden opportunity to show how good you are, and there is evidence to suggest that a customer whose complaint is dealt with well becomes a more loyal customer than one who has never had cause to complain. However, a complaint handled badly will result in a customer feeling even more angry than over the original cause and will guarantee that they meet their target of telling at least 10 other customers or potential customers about their experiences!

The golden rules for handling complaints are listed below.

- Make it *easy* for customers to complain. Is it clear to whom they should complain? Must they do so in writing? It is surprising how many organisations still insist on this. Many customers would consider it was adding insult to injury to have to take time to write a letter after the inconvenience they have already suffered.

■ Make sure customers feel their complaints are *welcomed*. Show that you are pleased they have taken the time and trouble to make the complaint. Consider having signs up encouraging customers to complain if they are not happy.

▲ If customers are making the complaint verbally, remember the rules for developing *positive relationships*: build and maintain rapport; listen actively; question effectively. People often find it difficult to complain: they suspect they are going to receive an unfriendly response. Often, anger over what has happened is compounded by the fear of a negative reaction. So, sometimes customers come across more strongly than they intend – see some tips in the table on page 56 for dealing with these situations.

● Respond *quickly* to complaints, even if it is just a holding letter to say the complaint is being investigated. Often organisations set standards, such as 'all customer complaints must have a response within two days'. However, do not make the mistake, having sent off a holding letter, of letting a resolution of the complaint drag on. If it is a very complex problem, write again explaining the delay: *keep the customer informed*.

● Seek *information* from all relevant sources eg what really did happen during the delivery, what alternative models there are to the damaged camera, how quickly a replacement can be obtained.

● Generate *alternative solutions* for customers: it is helpful to offer a choice.

■ Give customers the *benefit of the doubt*: it is often impossible to get to the bottom of complaints.

▲ Be *generous* in your response: if the customer has a genuine complaint you need to put it right and consider offering some form of compensation for the inconvenience or upset caused. Make sure that the offer is appropriate, or it can do more harm than good.

● Try to *exceed customers' expectations*. For example, we once had a problem with an order of wallpaper. We went in to collect it but the rolls could not be found, although they were shown as in stock. The manager of the department delivered it personally the same day on his way home at 8.30 pm. We were impressed!

● Always *do what you say you will do*. Make an action plan: what action needs to be taken? Who is involved? When will it take place? What resources will be needed? Check that all actions have been taken.

● *Check* that the customer is happy with the outcome.

■ *Learn* from complaints: make records of the complaints and their solutions, pass details of recurring complaints and/or problems to appropriate colleagues, identify potential new ways for resolving customer complaints and explain/review these with appropriate colleagues. (This is all about systems and procedures, which are

Ten tips for dealing with customer complaints

1 *Let the customer have their say*. When someone is angry or upset it is helpful for them to have the opportunity to 'let off steam'. It also indicates to the customer that you are willing to take the time to listen.

2 *Say you are sorry to hear what has happened*. This does not mean you are admitting that you or your organisation are in the wrong, but that you are sorry the customer thinks this is the case and is upset.

3 *Listen actively*. Show that you are listening; to check your understanding reflect back what has been said.

4 *Get at the facts by questioning effectively*. Make sure you get to the heart of the problem. Often there can be more than one problem – make sure you get to all of them. Remember that the customer may not always voice them in order of importance.

5 *Keep an open mind*. Do not make assumptions.

6 *Do not argue or be defensive*. Concentrate on the situation, not the personalities.

7 *Try to find out what outcome the customer wants*. Do they want a replacement cooker, their money back or to have their existing cooker mended but with some allowance on the price? Try to build on the customer's ideas and suggestions.

8 *Concentrate on what you can do and explain what you cannot do*. For example: 'I can arrange a service visit tomorrow. It is not possible today because all the experienced fitters are out on jobs today.'

9 *Do not impose your own solution*. You must reach a solution that the customer finds acceptable.

10 *Always summarise and check that the customer understands and agrees*. It is often helpful to follow this up in writing.

covered in the next chapter.) *It is essential that every complaint is seen as an opportunity to learn about customer needs and to adapt and improve the service/product the better to meet those needs.*

We generally think of customer complaints in terms of the external customer, yet the principles for handling internal customer complaints are just the same. However, there are some differences as well. Many complaints from internal customers are handled informally as part of the normal working relationship, and there are often no systems for monitoring such complaints. Therefore the opportunity to learn from them may be lost. A possible exception to this is the Staff Grievance Procedure, which allows staff to register a 'customer complaint' about how they have been treated by the organisation. Just like external customers, some internal customers may be loath to complain in case it results in unpleasantness and, again just like external customers, are left feeling aggrieved. However, the spin-off effects can be even more serious than for external customers, because they may significantly hinder effective teamworking. Spend a few minutes either on your own or with your team, thinking about how well you:

- encourage your colleagues and/or staff to complain or (perhaps to use a more friendly term) provide feedback on your services to them

- deal with that feedback in terms of taking action

- monitor and record the feedback so as to learn from it.

Finally, remember that customer complaints, be they internal or external, are an excellent opportunity to get really close to your customers and show them what you can do. In Jan Carlson's terms these are the *critical* 'moments of truth' – those superb opportunities to convert an unhappy customer into a customer for life. Make the most of them, in every sense.

Reference

1   PETERS T. J. *and* WATERMAN R. H. JNR. *In Search of Excellence: Lessons from America's best-run companies.* New York, Harper & Row, 1982.

customer-focused systems and procedures

Purpose of systems and procedures

Systems and procedures help organisations work in an efficient and effective way. Usually sets of rules or ways of doing things, they often involve the use of standard forms; these days computers also play an increasingly important role. In large organisations, systems and procedures are more formalised to ensure consistency of working, whereas in smaller organisations they may be simpler and more informal.

Systems and procedures are there to help and serve staff to ensure the customer receives the best possible service. They should always be focused on, and driven by, customer need. However, there is always a danger that systems and procedures develop a life of their own and become the master rather than the servant. Problems can arise because they:

● are usually, almost by definition, inflexible – they set out the right way of doing some activity.

■ do not cope well with unusual situations – customers' needs that do not fit the traditional mould eg a customer wanting to buy one glass normally sold as part of a set, or a customer wanting a delivery at an unusual time.

are often used as an excuse for not trying to meet customers' needs eg 'the system won't allow me to do it that way' or 'the system always takes three days and there is nothing I can do to intervene'. (Do these sound familiar?)

● are often blamed for inadequacies in the service eg 'we have not got any in stock – it's the stock ordering system, it's always going wrong'.

● tend to get set in tablets of stone and not respond to changes in the needs of customers or the organisation. This is often because it can take a lot of time, money and other resources to change a system or procedure.

● become so familiar that people are unable to think of other and better ways of doing things.

The golden rule with systems and procedures is to ask the following questions *all* the time:

● How do they help the customer?

■ Are they as relevant to the customers' needs today as when they were set up?

▲ How could they be changed to improve customer service?

Do not be complacent about your systems and procedures. We would suggest that few could not be improved!

Impact of information technology

The use of information technology has transformed many systems and procedures and had a major impact on the service offered to the customer. Let's look at some examples:

- *Check-out tills*: these scan goods (allowing quicker throughput and fewer mistakes), provide itemised bills (helping customers check their purchases), re-order stock automatically, print cheques and swipe debit cards (making payment quicker and easier).

- *Automatic Teller Machines (ATMs)*: 'holes in the wall' where customers can withdraw or deposit money and get account balances. These open up banking to 24-hour service.

- *Customer databases*: these allow customer details to be held and accessed in a variety of ways, making deliveries, invoicing and marketing more efficient.

- *Electronic mail (e-mail)*: this enables immediate communication within and between organisations eg with suppliers and customers.

Information technology will continue to have a major impact on the quality of customer service. However, there is a danger that sometimes the systems are designed without the customer sufficiently in mind: for example, a booking system for flights that cannot cope with special requirements, such as particular dietary needs, or does not allow for booking of non-smoking seats; or ticket machines with poor instructions. Another downside is that sometimes such systems completely remove the human element, as ATMs do, or significantly reduce it, for example when check-out operators get obsessed with their scanners and cheque-writing machines and forget about the customer. Beware of this!

Types of systems and procedures

There is a vast range of systems and procedures in organisations. Each will have as an end-user of the process a customer – either internal (eg served by the financial reporting system) or external (eg served by the delivery system). *Ultimately, however, all systems and procedures impact on the external customer.* For example, external customers will not be directly involved in the stock ordering system, but are affected by whether stock is available when they need it.

However, let's look first at the systems and procedures that impact most directly on the external customer. These are

- sales and ordering systems
- accounts and invoice systems
- delivery systems
- after-sales service systems
- customer complaint systems.

The table opposite sets out the sorts of questions you need to ask constantly about these systems to ensure they are customer-focused.

Questioning the external customer systems

Systems	Questions
Sales and order systems	– How easy is it for a customer to make a purchase or place an order: how long does it take; what does the customer have to do?
	– What confirmation does the customer receive: how easy is it for the customer to understand and check; how long after the order is placed does the confirmation arrive?
	– How is the customer kept informed about their order: how regularly; do you provide explanations for delays?
	– How quickly is an order processed: are there any ways it can be speeded up?
	– How flexible is the system: how does it deal with non-standard requests; urgent orders?
Accounts and invoice systems	– How accurate are the invoices?
	– How easy is it for a customer to query an invoice?
	– How easy is it for the customer to pay – in terms of methods of payment?
	– What credit arrangements are available: how does the customer find out about them; how good is the information; what does the customer need to do?
Delivery systems	– How flexible is the system in meeting customers' needs eg will you deliver when customers want, or only according to fixed schedules; will you give a specific time or only am/pm?
	– How do you inform the customer about deliveries: is it clear what the arrangements are and how they can be queried or amended; how much notice do you give?

Systems	Questions
Delivery systems *(cont)*	– How reliable is the system: do deliveries happen at the time expected; are the right goods/all the goods delivered; are they in perfect condition?
	– What sort of quality checks are made: are the goods checked before delivery/on delivery?
After-sales service systems	– How easy is it for customers to make contact: how do customers know whom to contact; what are your opening hours; what happens outside those hours?
	– How flexible is the system to meet the customers' needs eg will a service engineer come when the customer wants or according to fixed visiting schedules; will you give a specific time or only am/pm?
	– How quickly does the system respond: how long does a customer have to wait for a service engineer's call or a spare part?
	– How well does the system follow-up eg need for more visits; co-ordinating spare parts availability with engineers' visits?
Customer complaint systems	– How easy is it for customers to complain: is it clear whom they should complain to; must complaints be in writing?
	– How quickly do you respond with holding letters? How quickly do you resolve problems?
	– How well does the system follow-up: do you check with customers that complaints have been resolved; do you take any action required within the organisation?
	– How well does the system monitor and analyse complaints: who receives the information; in what form; how is it used?

Next let's look at systems that impact primarily on the internal customers eg those you use in order to obtain a piece of office furniture, book a room for a meeting, get information on expenditure against budget or book a place on a training course. With some of these systems you will be the customer and with others the supplier. How well do these systems meet their customers' needs? Take the last example of booking a place on a training course – you could ask exactly the same questions as those posed for the sales and order systems in the table on pages 63–4.

A very important system is that concerned with holding information on the products/services offered and on the customers themselves. It is vital that the information is accurate, up to date and accessible. This means that the methods used to capture the data must be reliable and the system robust enough to deal with peak workloads. Another key issue is confidentiality and security. This is particularly important when dealing with customer information held on computers because, as with any other computerised source of information on individuals, these systems are covered by the Data Protection Act.

Having thought about systems both for external and internal customers, try Exercise 7 overleaf.

Exercise 7

Choose two systems or procedures that are important to you or
your team's work where:

⊙ you or your team are the initiator or supplier
▣ you or your team are the customer.

Analyse these systems in terms of how well they meet customer
needs. This makes a good exercise for a training programme or
team briefing session.

System	What works well?	What does not work well?	How could the system be improved?

Finally, remember that systems and procedures are there to
serve your customers – make sure yours do!

6 continuously improving customer care

What does it mean?

Many customer care initiatives start off with a 'big bang' involving mission and value statements, training programmes, and new systems and procedures, the latter often linked to the organisation's seeking to achieve standards such as BS 5750 or ISO 9000. However, it is widely accepted now that the path to organisational excellence is not achieved by one-off initiatives, but involves a continuous process of improvement. With customer care it involves every individual continuously striving to improve the services they, their team and their organisation offer.

The process of making continuous improvements to customer service is often known as *Kaizen*, a Japanese term. *Kai* in Japanese means 'change', and *zen* means 'good' or 'for the better'. *Kaizen* therefore means, literally, 'change for the better'. Although the application of Kaizen originated in manufacturing, it is now acknowledged as a technique that can be used in all types of organisations and processes. The principle underpinning Kaizen is that processes and systems should be driven by a powerful focus on the (internal and external) customer need. Everyone involved in the process is encouraged constantly to seek and maintain small, easily accomplished improvements. To be successful, it depends critically on three factors. There must be:

● a clear understanding of what the organisation wants to achieve

■ two-way communication that is open and runs throughout the organisation

▲ a commitment to feed back constantly on the effects of the improvements.

Kaizen is not in itself, perhaps surprisingly, results-oriented; it is unreservedly process-oriented. The philosophy is that by getting the processes right, other things (eg results) fall naturally into place. It is in essence:

● a variety of techniques combined to produce results that in themselves may be trivial but that together deliver considerable improvements

■ based on the assumption that the whole improvement in customer care as a result of these minor changes is greater than the sum of the parts

▲ people-based, recognising that those actually doing the job, who are nearest to the 'action', know most about what is going on, and are best placed to identify improvements required and to take action

● team-oriented, emphasising the importance of teams

working together so that improvements can be co-ordinated

● a way of delivering high-quality customer care through attention to fine detail.

How does continuous improvement work?

There are three key ingredients:

● *Knowing what you are trying to achieve.* Mission and value statements set out the organisation's goals and objectives – these then need to be translated into performance standards for everyone in the organisation.

■ *Knowing how you are doing.* You need information on whether you are meeting the performance standards, on what customers think about the service you are offering.

▲ *Taking action continuously to improve the care you offer.* There is no point in having the first two ingredients unless you, your team and organisation are willing to act on the information.

Performance/service standards

Knowing what you are trying to achieve can be tackled at various levels. Many people will have a job description setting out the purpose of the job and the tasks involved. What is sometimes difficult to set out are the standards to which the job should be done. At the heart of continuous improvement is the availability of clear, objective performance/service standards for all staff, balancing the needs of customers and the organisation. Examples of typical performance/service standards used in customer care are:

- telephone calls to be answered within three rings

- queues at checkouts to have no more than two people

- pizzas to be delivered within 45 minutes of the order

- quarterly budget report to be completed within one week of the end of the quarter

- service calls to be made within 15 minutes of the time agreed with the customer.

A number of organisations now embody performance standards within so-called Customer Charters, often with compensation promised if standards are not met. For example, London Underground Ltd (LUL) promised in 1994 that 'If, because of our failure, you wait on a platform for more than 15 minutes longer than advertised, or the Underground train you are on is delayed by 15 minutes, we will refund you with a voucher to the value of the delayed single journey.'[1] The philosophy of continuous improvement would also mean that the standards themselves are being raised continuously, eg the LUL standard in 1992 had been 20 minutes.

Measuring your performance

The more difficult standards are where it is hard to quantify and measure the level of performance required eg friendly and courteous service or handling complaints so well that the customer wishes to return and use your services again. It is possible to devise some quantifiable measures eg numbers of complaints or amount of repeat business. However, the most direct, and key, measure is the customer's perceptions of what occurred: did the customer care meet the customer's expectation and (hopefully) exceed it?

So how do we find out? Be creative and think of as many ways as possible. Examples could include:

- customer comment cards

- customer surveys – these can take a variety of forms eg interview surveys, where an interviewer will go out and talk to a cross-section of customers, or self-complete questionnaires sent out to all, or a sample of, customers

- ▲ 'mystery customers' – covertly checking and reporting back on the service

- telephoning customers after the event

- asking customers at the time

- listening to, and observing, customers.

The last example is very important: if you use all the communication skills described in Chapter 3, you will *know* whether your customer is satisfied. One of the best sources of information on customer needs and perceptions is the person who actually deals with the customer. He or she will know whether the customer is happy, which aspects of the service are really important to the customer, which aspects niggle the customer. A hotel we stayed at recently used a public car park for resident's parking, but the customer was required to return to the car each day to put another daily parking ticket on the windscreen. This was a serious inconvenience, so we made our views known to the receptionist who provided the parking ticket. But did this important customer feedback ever get recorded or acted upon?

A key issue here is how to capture all this valuable information. Again, be creative. Think about:

- setting up a 'wow' board to record those things that went really well, and a 'groan' board to record the things that did not

- having a slot during regular team briefing sessions to discuss customer reactions. For this to work the sessions need to be frequent, probably weekly, so that memories are fresh.

- encouraging staff to complete a form to record the 'wows' and the 'groans' – but make sure it is simple and quick to complete.

Above all, encourage staff to be aware of all aspects of the service they provide and its impact on their customers, and to be honest with themselves, their colleagues and their managers. However, remember that nobody is going to report 'groans' if they think they will be judged and penalised. Equally important is to encourage staff to think of solutions, not just present the problems – they will almost certainly know best!

Some organisations use suggestion schemes, where staff submit ideas on how the organisation could improve its products and service. Often there are rewards for ideas that are adopted. Such schemes can be very useful, but they do not always pick up the everyday, often small and detailed issues that can cumulatively provide such a wealth of information on how to improve your customer care.

Taking action

The last key step is ensuring action is taken. There are three types of situation:

● The individual member of staff can think of appropriate solutions eg changes in procedures and is personally able to implement them.

■ The issues relate to the team, and the team or team leader has the authority to take action.

▲ The issues go wider than the immediate team, or the changes are sufficiently major, so as to require approval at a higher level.

Empowerment is a concept that is being discussed in many organisations. In very simple terms, it means both allowing and enabling individuals or teams to take as many decisions and actions as possible themselves without seeking further authority. For empowerment to be successful the limits of individual authority have to be clear eg on giving refunds or changing procedures, and the organisation has to be tolerant of mistakes or misjudgements. It is a powerful concept in the process of Kaizen, because it shortens the chain between an improvement being identified and action being taken. Clearly, there are limits to which an employee might be empowered to make changes to expensive machinery or complex business systems, especially where the procedure is documented for BS 5750 or ISO 9000. At the very least he or she should be empowered to 'blow the whistle' on anything that is not working as it should.

A risk with shortening the information-to-action chain is that chances may take place that affect other key members in the process. It is important to think through any changes by asking:

- who needs to be consulted – within your team, your organisation or outside the organisation (eg suppliers)

- who needs to be informed of the changes – within your team, your organisation or outside the organisation (eg customers).

Try Exercise 8 on page 76 to determine how well your organisation is set up to make continuous improvements.

How did you fare in Exercise 8? Are you able to make improvements to the processes or make suggestions for such improvements? Are these suggestions/improvements well received by your organisation? Do you get regular feedback?

There is growing evidence that continuous improvement in customer care, whether internal or external, is essential to the success of organisations. What are *you* going to do to ensure that you, your team and your organisation achieve the goal of excellent customer care?

Reference

1   LONDON UNDERGROUND LTD. *London Underground's 1994 Customer Charter*. London, LUL, 1994.

Exercise 8

Does your organisation encourage continuous improvement?

Answer the following questions by circling the answer that is correct for you.

1 Are there clear performance standards for your job?	Yes / No / Sometimes
2 Are you regularly provided with information on your results?	Yes / No / Sometimes
3 Are you empowered to make changes to the procedures?	Yes / No / Sometimes
4 Do you make changes to the procedures?	Yes / No / Sometimes
5 Do you ever have ideas for improvements for which you are not empowered to make changes?	Yes / No / Sometimes
6 Do you feel able to make suggestions for these improvements?	Yes / No / Sometimes
7 Are these suggestions welcomed by your immediate boss?	Yes / No / Sometimes
8 Does anything happen as a result of your suggestions?	Yes / No / Sometimes
9 Are you told what has happened to your suggestions?	Yes / No / Sometimes
10 Are you thanked for making the suggestions?	Yes / No / Sometimes

If you score 10 'yes' answers you are well positioned to make continuous improvements to your customer care. A mixture of 'yes' and 'sometimes' answers suggest that you are in a reasonable position to make continuous improvements. However, if you score 10, or close on 10, 'no' answers perhaps there needs to be an improvement in the 'customer' care you receive before you will be able to make any serious continuous improvements of your own.

appendices

Useful videos

There is a wide range of useful videos on customer care, and more are coming out all the time. Here is a selection of those currently available:

If Looks Could Kill: The power of behaviour, from Video Arts.

Telephone Behaviour: The power and perils, from Video Arts.

Frontline Customer Care, from Fenman.

Colleagues as Customers, from Fenman.

Managing for Customer Care, from Fenman.

No Complaints? (two videos), from Video Arts

Further reading

CARR C. *Front-line Customer Service: 15 keys to customer satisfaction*. New York, John Wiley & Sons, 1990.

CLUTTERBUCK D., CLARK G., *and* ARMISTEAD C. *Inspired Customer Service: Strategies for service quality*. London, Kogan Page, 1993.

KING TAYLOR L. *Quality: Total customer service*. London, Century Business, 1992.

LASH L. M. *The Complete Guide to Customer Service*. New York, John Wiley & Sons, 1989.

MACKAY I. *Asking Questions*. 2nd edn. London, Institute of Personnel and Development, 1995.

MACKAY I. *Listening Skills*. 2nd edn. London, Institute of Personnel and Development, 1995.

With over 90,000 members, the **Institute of Personnel and Development** is the largest organisation in Europe dealing with the management and development of people. The IPD operates its own publishing unit, producing books and research reports for human resource practitioners, students, and general managers charged with people-management responsibilities.

Currently there are over 160 titles covering the full range of personnel and development issues. The books have been commissioned from leading experts in the field and are packed with the latest information and guidance on best practice.

For free copies of the IPD Books Catalogue, please contact the publishing department:

Tel.: 0181-263 3387
Fax: 0181-263 3850
E-mail: publish@ipd.co.uk
Web: http://www.ipd.co.uk

Orders for books should be sent to:

Plymbridge Distributors
Estover
Plymouth
Devon
PL6 7PZ

(Credit card orders) Tel.: 01752 202 301
Fax: 01752 202 333

Upcoming titles in the *Management Shapers* series

Publication: March 1999

Body Language at Work
Adrian Furnham
ISBN 0 85292 771 1

Introducing NLP
Sue Knight
ISBN 0 85292 772 X

Learning for Earning
Eric Parsloe and Caroline Allen
ISBN 0 85292 774 6

Motivating People

Iain Maitland

Will help you maximise individual and team skills to achieve personal, departmental and, above all, organisational goals. It provides practical insights into:

- becoming a better leader and co-ordinating winning teams

- identifying, setting and communicating achievable targets

- empowering others through simple job improvement techniques

- encouraging self-development, defining training needs and providing helpful assessment

- ensuring that pay and workplace conditions make a positive contribution to satisfaction and commitment.

1998 96 pages   ISBN 0 85292 766 5

Negotiating, Persuading and Influencing

Alan Fowler

Develop the skills you need to manage your staff effectively, bargain successfully with colleagues or deal tactfully with superiors. Sound advice on:

- probing and questioning techniques

- timing your tactics and using adjournments

- conceding and compromising to find common ground

- resisting manipulative ploys

- securing and implementing agreement.

1998 96 pages   ISBN 085292 755 X

Working in Teams

Alison Hardingham

Looks at teamworking from the inside. It will give you valuable insights into how you can make a more positive and effective contribution – as team member or team leader – to ensure that your team works together and achieves together. Clear and practical guidelines are given on:

- understanding the nature and make-up of teams

- finding out if your team is on track

- overcoming the most common teamworking problems

- recognising your own strengths and weaknesses as a team member

- giving teams the tools, techniques and organisational support they need.

1998 96 pages   ISBN 0 85292 767 3

Other titles in the *Management Shapers* series

All titles are priced at £5.95 (£5.36 to IPD members)

The Appraisal Discussion

Terry Gillen

Shows you how to make appraisal a productive and motivating experience for all levels of performer. It includes:

- ● assessing performance fairly and accurately

- ■ using feedback to improve performance

- ▲ handling reluctant appraisees and avoiding bias

- ◉ agreeing future objectives

- ● identifying development needs.

1998 96 pages   ISBN 0 85292 751 7

Asking Questions

Ian MacKay

Will help you ask the 'right' questions, using the correct form to elicit a useful response. All managers need to hone their questioning skills, whether interviewing, appraising or simply exchanging ideas. This book offers guidance and helpful advice on:

- using various forms of open question – including probing, simple interrogative, opinion-seeking, hypothetical, extension and precision etc

- encouraging and drawing out speakers through supportive statements and interjections

- establishing specific facts through closed or 'direct' approaches

- avoiding counter-productive questions

- using questions in a training context.

1998 96 pages   ISBN 0 85292 768 1

Assertiveness

Terry Gillen

Will help you feel naturally confident, enjoy the respect of others and easily establish productive working relationships, even with 'awkward' people. It covers:

- understanding why you behave as you do and, when that behaviour is counter-productive, knowing what to do about it

- understanding other people better

- keeping your emotions under control

- preventing others' bullying, flattering or manipulating you

- acquiring easy-to-learn techniques that you can use immediately

- developing your personal assertiveness strategy.

1998 96 pages   ISBN 0 85292 769 X

The Disciplinary Interview

Alan Fowler

This book will ensure that you adopt the correct procedures, conduct productive interviews and manage the outcome with confidence. It includes:

- ● understanding the legal implications
- ■ probing the employee's case and defusing conflict
- ▲ weighing up the alternatives to dismissal.

1998 96 pages   ISBN 0 85292 753 3

Leadership Skills

John Adair

Will give you confidence and guide and inspire you on your journey from being an effective manager to becoming a leader of excellence. Adair offers stimulating insights into:

- ● recognising and developing your leadership qualities
- ■ acquiring the personal authority to give positive direction and the flexibility to embrace change
- ▲ acting on the key interacting needs – to achieve your task, build your team, and develop its members.

1998 96 pages   ISBN 0 85292 764 9

Motivating People

Iain Maitland

Will help you maximise individual and team skills to achieve personal, departmental and, above all, organisational goals. It provides practical insights into:

- becoming a better leader and co-ordinating winning teams
- identifying, setting and communicating achievable targets
- empowering others through simple job improvement techniques
- encouraging self-development, defining training needs and providing helpful assessment
- ensuring that pay and workplace conditions make a positive contribution to satisfaction and commitment.

1998 96 pages   ISBN 0 85292 766 5

Listening Skills

Ian MacKay

(Second Edition)

Improve your ability in this crucial management skill! Clear explanations will help you:

- recognise the inhibitors to listening

- listen to what is really being said by analysing and evaluating the message

- interpret tone of voice and non-verbal signals.

1998 80 pages   ISBN 0 85292 754 1

Making Meetings Work

Patrick Forsyth

Will maximise your time (both before and during meetings), clarify your aims, improve your own and others' performance and make the whole process rewarding and productive. The book is full of practical tips and advice on:

- drawing up objectives and setting realistic agendas

- deciding the who, where, and when to meet

- chairing effectively – encouraging discussion, creativity and sound decision-making

- sharpening your skills of observation, listening and questioning to get your points across

1998 96 pages   ISBN 0 85292 765 7